Steer Wrestling

By John Hamilton

Visit us at
www.abdopublishing.com

Published by ABDO Publishing Company, PO Box 398166, Minneapolis, MN 55439. Copyright ©2014 by Abdo Consulting Group, Inc. International copyrights reserved in all countries. No part of this book may be reproduced in any form without written permission from the publisher. A&D Xtreme™ is a trademark and logo of ABDO Publishing Company.

Printed in the United States of America, North Mankato, Minnesota.
052013
092013

 PRINTED ON RECYCLED PAPER

Editor: Sue Hamilton
Graphic Design: John Hamilton
Cover: John Hamilton
Photos: All photos by John Hamilton, except: Library of Congress-pg 8; Getty Images, pg 9.

ABDO Booklinks
Web sites about rodeos are featured on our Book Links pages. These links are routinely monitored and updated to provide the most current information available. Web site: www.abdopublishing.com

Library of Congress Control Number: 2013931683

Cataloging-in-Publication Data

Hamilton, John.
 Steer wrestling / John Hamilton.
   p. cm. -- (Xtreme rodeo)
ISBN 978-1-61783-981-8
1. Steer wrestling--Juvenile literature.   I. Title.
791.8/4--dc23
                                    2013931683

Contents

Steer Wrestling 4

History 8

The Start 10

The Hazer 12

The Grab 14

The Throw 20

Scoring 22

Equipment 24

Injuries 26

Steers 28

Glossary 30

Index 32

Steer Wrestling

Steer wrestling takes equal parts strength and finesse. Cowboys describe the sport as like driving a pickup truck at 30 miles per hour (48 kph), leaping out the window, and tackling a mailbox. Except in the case of bulldoggers, they're actually grabbing onto a 500-pound (227-kg) steer in full stride.

Steer wrestlers are known as bulldoggers (steers are called "doggies").

5

Steer wrestling is a timed rodeo event. Cowboys compete against the clock and themselves. The goal is to wrestle a running steer to the ground. The cowboy with the fastest time wins. It sounds like a simple contest, but it is much more difficult than it seems. Steers are strong and fast, and too big for most cowboys to overpower. Only the best can compete and win. Champion bulldoggers usually finish the job in three or four seconds.

History

Steer wrestling is the only rodeo event that doesn't have its roots in real-life ranch work. Cowboy Bill Pickett is usually credited with starting steer wrestling in the early 1900s at Wild West shows.

Bill Pickett is the first African American to be inducted into the National Cowboy & Western Heritage Museum's Rodeo Hall of Fame.

The Start

Steer wrestling begins with the cowboy on horseback waiting in a fenced area called the "box." A breakaway rope barrier is placed in front of the box. The steer waits in a narrow steel-tubed enclosure called a "chute." When the cowboy nods his head, spring-loaded doors on the chute open and the steer bursts into the arena.

Rope barrier

Chute

The steer is always given a head start. When the rope barrier on the box drops, the cowboy and his horse bolt out of the box and chase the steer.

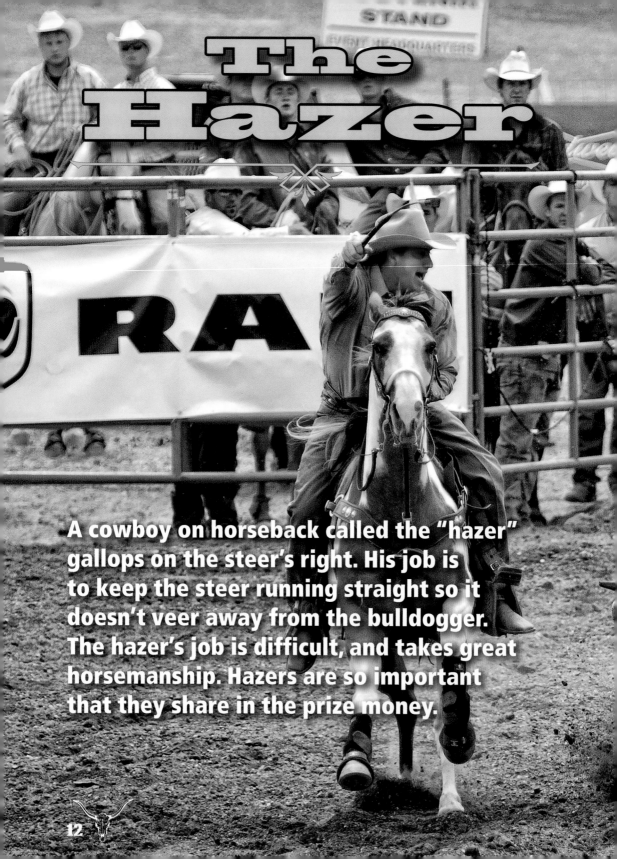

The Hazer

A cowboy on horseback called the "hazer" gallops on the steer's right. His job is to keep the steer running straight so it doesn't veer away from the bulldogger. The hazer's job is difficult, and takes great horsemanship. Hazers are so important that they share in the prize money.

13

The Grab

When the bulldogger's horse catches up to the steer, the bulldogger leans down to his right and eases out of the saddle. In midair, he grabs the steer's left horn with his left hand. Simultaneously, he hooks his right arm around the animal's right horn.

Steers weigh more than twice as much as the cowboys. To bring them to a stop requires great technique and power. After grabbing the steer's horns, the bulldogger digs his heels into the dirt. If he loses his balance or leans too far forward or back, he could be thrown under the steer and trampled.

17

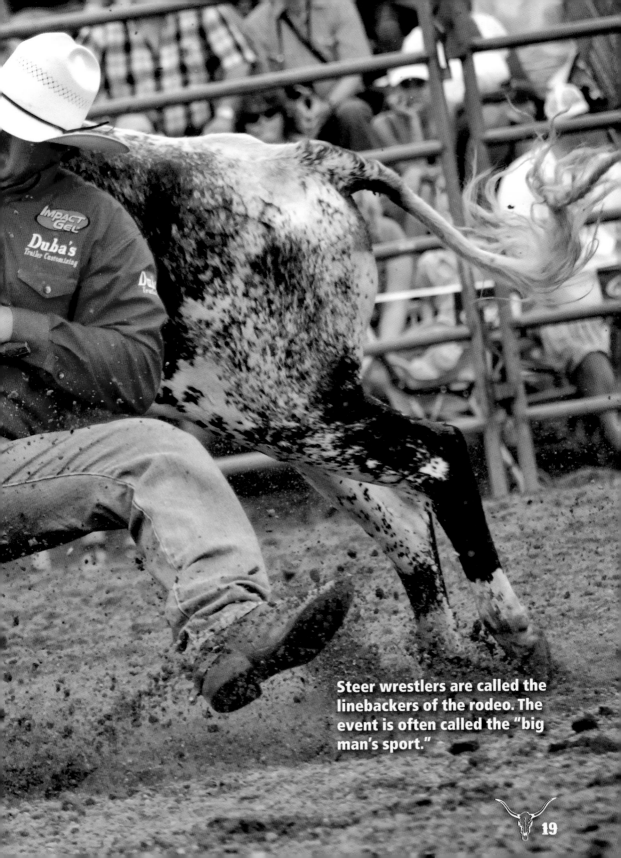

Steer wrestlers are called the linebackers of the rodeo. The event is often called the "big man's sport."

The Throw

After slowing the steer down, the bulldogger cups the steer's head in the crook of his arms and twists. The animal is thrown off balance and its body arcs. The bulldogger leans back with the steer's head firmly in his grasp, which forces it to hit the ground. If it falls flat with all four hooves pointed in the same direction, an official waves a red flag and the timer stops.

The bulldogger keeps a firm grip on the steer's head and twists.

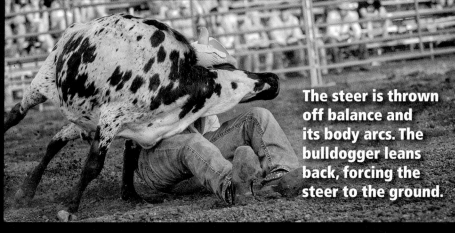

The steer is thrown off balance and its body arcs. The bulldogger leans back, forcing the steer to the ground.

When the steer hits the ground fast with all four legs in the same direction, it is called a "pancake."

The cowboy checks his time.

Scoring

Steer wrestling is a timed event, and scoring is simple. The timer starts when the bulldogger's horse comes out of the box. It stops when the bulldogger has thrown the steer on its side, with all four legs pointed in one direction. If the horse leaves the box early, a 10-second penalty is added.

Equipment

There is no special equipment required for steer wrestling. The dress code of most professional rodeos requires jeans, a long-sleeved shirt, and a Western-style hat and boots. Besides those items, all a bulldogger needs is years of practice, strong muscles, and expert timing.

Injuries

Steer wrestlers stretch their muscles before each event. But even after properly warming up, injuries can still occur. The most common injury is to a cowboy's knees, which take a beating when trying to slow down the freight-train-like animal. Sometimes bulldoggers are injured by a steer's horns or hooves. Bruised shins are also common.

Steers

A steer is a male calf that has been castrated at an early age, unlike a bull. Most rodeo steers are between 12 and 15 months old. They must weigh at least 500 pounds (227 kg) and have horns at least eight inches (20 cm) long. Injuries to the steers are very rare. The Corriente steers used in rodeos have good endurance and an easy temperament.

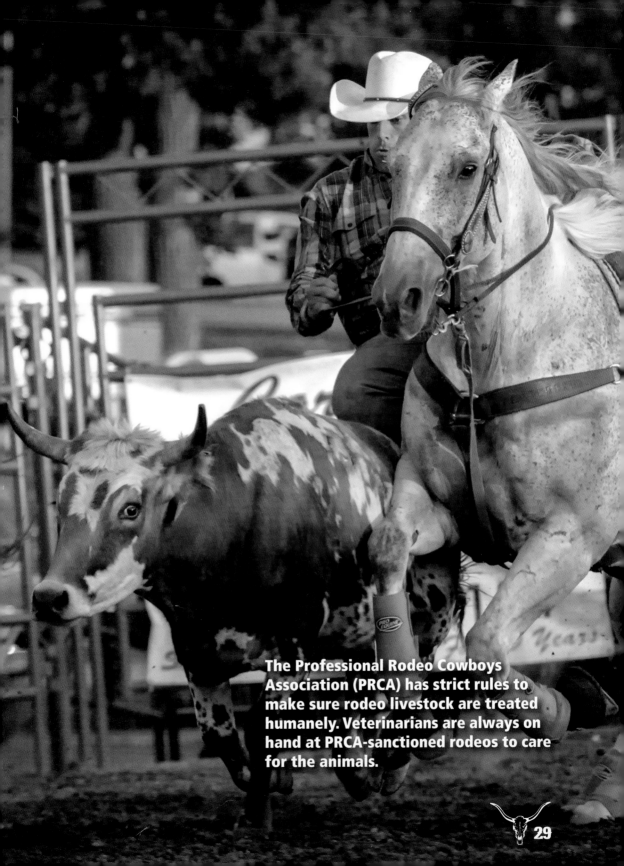

The Professional Rodeo Cowboys Association (PRCA) has strict rules to make sure rodeo livestock are treated humanely. Veterinarians are always on hand at PRCA-sanctioned rodeos to care for the animals.

Glossary

Bulldoggers

Rodeo cowboys who compete in the steer wrestling event. Also called the linebackers of the rodeo.

Castrated

When a male animal has its testes surgically removed. Also called neutering. Steers are male calves that have been castrated. Steers are not as large or aggressive as bulls, which are not castrated.

Corriente Steer

Most rodeo steers are Corriente steers. They are somewhat small, athletic, with upcurving horns, and have good endurance.

Professional Rodeo Cowboys Association

The world's largest and oldest rodeo sanctioning organization. It ensures that rodeos meet high standards in working conditions and livestock welfare. Located in Colorado Springs, Colorado, it sanctions about 600 rodeos in the U.S. and Canada.

Timed Event

A rodeo event, such as steer wrestling, in which contestants compete against the clock and themselves. The other kind of rodeo contest is the roughstock event, such as bull riding, which pits human versus animal.

Wild West Shows

Traveling shows, similar to circuses, that featured Western culture and contests, including rodeo events. They were very popular in the late 1800s and early 1900s. The most famous was Buffalo Bill's Wild West, featuring William "Buffalo Bill" Cody.

Index

B
"big man's sport" 19
box 10, 11, 22
breakaway rope
  barrier 10, 11
bulldogger 4, 5, 6, 12,
  14, 16, 20, 21, 22, 24,
  26

C
chute 10
Corriente steer 28

D
doggies 5

H
hazer 12

N
National Cowboy &
  Western Heritage
  Museum 9

P
pancake 21
Pickett, Bill 8, 9
Professional
  Rodeo Cowboys
  Association (PRCA)
  29

R
Rodeo Hall of Fame 9

S
saddle 14

steer 4, 5, 6, 10, 11,
  12, 14, 16, 20, 21, 22,
  26

T
timed event 22

V
veterinarian 29

W
Wild West show 8

Rodeo announcer Davie Kimm.